Puppy Problems

By Suzanne Weyn
Illustrated by Lee Pai

Scott Foresman
is an imprint of

PEARSON

Glenview, Illinois • Boston, Massachusetts • Chandler, Arizona •
Upper Saddle River, New Jersey

Illustrator Lee Pai

Photographs

Every effort has been made to secure permission and provide appropriate credit for photographic material. The publisher deeply regrets any omission and pledges to correct errors called to its attention in subsequent editions.

Unless otherwise acknowledged, all photographs are the property of Pearson Education, Inc.

20 ©RF Company/Alamy; **22** Gabe Palmer/Alamy Images.

ISBN 13: 987-0-328-51374-1
ISBN 10:   0-328-51374-1

2 3 4 5 6 7 8 9 10 V0N4 13 12 11 10

January 20, 3:00 p.m.

To: Hulahoopchamp

Hey, Lila!

Mom was sworn in as governor of the state this morning. The swearing-in ceremony was outside and, oh, was it ever cold! Mom wanted me to wear earmuffs, but I didn't want to. I didn't want all those newspaper photographers printing photos of me wearing earmuffs! How embarrassing!

Everyone will be watching everything I do now. I don't know if I can handle it. The good thing, though, is that Mom promised that as soon we moved into the Governor's Mansion, I'd get to have a puppy. Well now we're here, and the time has come. My lifelong dream of puppy ownership is finally coming true!

It's fun living in the Governor's Mansion, but I already miss you like crazy.

Zoë

January 20, 6:30 p.m.

To: Wannapuppy

Hi, Zoë!

I just saw you on the news! Way to go! The French braid looked awesome. Good thing you refused the earmuffs. It would have totally wrecked the look. Some things are worth fighting for.

Speaking of fighting, today Vinnie Petrotsky said you would become stuck up now that you live in the Governor's Mansion. Of course, I totally disagree and told him so right away. He kept insisting, but what does he know? Nothing!

What kind of dog are you going to get?

Lila

January 22, 3:35 p.m.

To: Wannapuppy

   Luck! Luck! Luck! That's me wishing you luck. Download a photo of the lucky pup that you select, and send it to me as soon as you can! I can't wait to see what you pick!

   L

January 22, 3:36 p.m.

To: Hulahoopchamp

   I'll do that as soon as I pick one. We're pulling up to the shelter now! Talk to you later!

January 22, 5:30 p.m.

To: Wannapuppy

   You forgot to send the photo. I bet you're busy playing with the puppy. I can't wait to see what it looks like. Send it as soon as you get this!

   L

January 23, 11:30 a.m.

To: Wannapuppy

Did you see the story about you in the newspaper? The headline says: GUV'S CARING KID TO PICK POUND PUP. Everyone approves, including me.

What is it like to have a new puppy? Are you showing it to the press? I'm still waiting for the photo. I don't want to be the last one to see your new dog.

L

January 23, 9:08 p.m.

To: Hulahoopchamp

Well, that was a disaster! The minute I got into the shelter, my eyes began watering. I started sneezing like crazy too. Then I broke out in a rash. It seems that I'm allergic to dogs. I never was allergic before, but I guess I haven't been near a dog in a while. I am so upset!

January 23, 9:15 p.m.

To: Wannapuppy

Have no fear! Your BFF Lila to the rescue! I did some research, and there are certain breeds of dogs that folks with allergies can have. These dogs don't have the allergens most dogs have. I am sending you a file that lists them. There are photos too.

January 23, 9:25 p.m.

To: Hulahoopchamp

You're a pal. These are adorable dogs. Do you think a shelter would have these?

Z

January 23, 9:35 p.m.

To: Wannapuppy

No. You have to get in touch with a dog breeder. These dogs are special breeds. Dogs like these cost a lot more than shelter dogs. But they're cute, and they won't make you sneeze. Ask your parents if you can have one of these.

Mom says I have to get off the computer now. Let me know what your parents say.

January 24, 3:25 p.m.

To: Hulahoopchamp

I'm going crazy! I want to ask Mom and Dad if we can get one of these special breeds, but Dad is still away, and Mom has been busy all day meeting with the teachers' union about education stuff. I got so frustrated that I talked to some reporters who were hanging around outside just to have someone to talk to.

Z

January 25, 9:31 a.m.

To: Wannapuppy

    I don't think you should have talked to those reporters yesterday about wanting a special purebred dog. Since you didn't mention it in your e-mail, I guess you haven't seen the newspaper today. I've cut and pasted the headline in here.

GUV'S SPOILED KID WANTS ONLY HIGH-PRICED PUREBRED POOCH!

    Ouch! Sorry to be the one to show you this. It's totally unfair.

    Vinnie Petrotsky said he told me so. I told him to leave me alone.

    Sincerely, your loyal friend, no matter what rotten things everyone says about you,

    L

January 25, 10:23 a.m.

To: Hulahoopchamp

You're not going to believe what is going on here this Saturday. When I woke up this morning, there were more than a hundred people in front of the mansion. At first, I thought they were the teachers' union having a rally to support education. But it wasn't the teachers. The people outside were all there to protest against me!

Me!

Mom rushed into my room telling me to hurry up and get dressed for a press conference.

"Wait! Wait!" I told her. "I don't want to talk to reporters. I just want a dog."

Mom said we had to show that we wished to be fair to all dogs and that, as a family, we would unite to handle this problem.

January 25, 12:00 p.m.

To: Wannapuppy

Zoë,

I just saw the press conference on TV. Wow! Those protesters were really mad at you! They kept chanting, "Get out of the fog! Adopt a dog!" so loudly. They didn't want to listen to what your Mom was saying about your allergies. You would have adopted a dog if they didn't make you sneeze. It took guts for you to stand there next to her and smile like that. I was very proud of you. I don't know if I could have been that brave.

January 25, 8:17 p.m.

To: Hulahoopchamp

What a day! Mom had to calm down all the pet shelters. Then the dog breeders started to call. They didn't like the press conference. They thought Mom was apologizing for wanting a purebred dog. They threatened to boycott every pet food company that donated money to Mom's election.

Mom had to make another public statement saying that anyone who wanted a purebred dog had every right to have one.

So now everyone is happy—except me. I still have no dog. Right now it looks like I'm never going to get one.

Z

January 25, 8:30 p.m.

To: Wannapuppy

I'll e-mail you tomorrow. I'm working on something right now. I hope it works.

L

January 26, 7:04 a.m.

To: Wannapuppy

Oh, yes! I'm a genius! I'm the best—if I do say so myself. I found what I was looking for last night. Click on the attachment to this e-mail, and tell me what you think.

January 26, 8:06 a.m.

To: Hulahoopchamp

Oh, he's *sooooo* cute! He's a purebred miniature schnauzer, AND he's in a shelter! Mom has already called the shelter and told them to hold him for us. I'm going right after school to get him! Mom says I have to spend an hour with him to make sure I'm able to be with him without sneezing or watering up.

He's not a puppy, but they say he's young. And who cares, anyway?

You're the best friend in the world!

Z

January 26, 7:00 p.m.

To: Wannapuppy

I saw you on the TV news this afternoon with Jack, your new dog! You both looked really happy, and I didn't even see you sniffle. (Like your new boots, BTW.)

Thanks for telling everyone it was me who found Jack online. It's a good thing pet shelters have Web sites you can check. It seems that dogs for people with allergies turn up in shelters all the time.

Vinnie Petrotsky says now that you said my name on TV, I'm going to get stuck up too. He invited me to his bowling birthday party this Saturday. Do you think I should go?

Can You Have a Dog if You're Allergic?

If you are allergic to dogs but would really like one as a pet, you do have some options.

Pick a breed of dog that produces fewer allergens, the small substances that cause an allergic reaction. Examples of these dogs include poodles, Airedales, and schnauzers.

Keep the dog out of your bedroom.

Wash your hands after playing with the dog.

Keep the house clean.

Some people think that a hairless dog is the answer to their allergy problems. In fact, dog allergens come from the dog's skin and saliva. Dogs that shed their hair frequently, however, are not the best choice. Allergens become trapped in the dog hair and can spread throughout the household.